I CAN'T FORGIVE

Jim Newcomer

Consulting Editor: Dr. Paul Tautges

Help! I Can't Forgive

© Jim Newcomer 2017

ISBN
Paper: 978-1-63342-069-4
ePub: ISBN 978-1-63342-070-0
Mobi: ISBN 978-1-63342-071-7

Published by **Shepherd Press**
P.O. Box 24
Wapwallopen, PA 18660

www.shepherdpress.com

All Scripture quotations are from the New American
Standard Bible (NASB). Copyright © 1995 by The
Lockman Foundation.

Printed in Colombia

Designed by **documen**

Contents

Introduction

Can you relate to this? The caller on the Christian radio program goes on for what seems like eternity, listing the many ways her father wronged her, years earlier. The husband of an unfaithful, albeit remorseful, wife confides with tears to his counselor that it is impossible to ever trust his wife and open his heart to her again. The pastor in the wake of a church split wonders how on earth he will ever find the strength to apply what he has for years preached on forgiveness.

Not a Solo but a Choir

What is the common refrain from this chorus of pained voices? "Help! We can't forgive!" We must admit that the struggle to forgive someone who has wronged us is universal. Indeed, the fight to forgive is "common to man" (1 Corinthians 10:13).

The factory default mode of every person is to be "unmerciful" (Romans 1:31). Sadly, this gravity of grudges is common in Christian circles as well. Jay Adams sees this clearly and writes with great honesty,

> *Forgiveness is the oil that keeps the machinery of the Christian home and church running smoothly.* ***In a world where even those who have been declared perfect in Christ sin, there is much to forgive****. Christians who must work together closely find themselves denting each others' fenders, now and then taking out a taillight or two, and at times even having head-on collisions. Under such conditions, forgiveness is what keeps things from breaking down completely [emphasis added].*[1]

Non-Forgivers Pay a High Price

If you are struggling with forgiving someone in your life, you are not alone ... even in the family

---

1   Jay Adams, *From Forgiven to Forgiving: Learning to Forgive One Another God's Way* (Amityville, NY: Calvary Press, 1994), 7.

of God, where believers are clearly encouraged to exist together in a culture of forgiveness (Ephesians 4:32; Colossians 3:13). Yet you must not allow the frequency of this struggle to be your excuse for being a non-forgiver. When Christians don't forgive, *it costs too much.* Just take a moment and consider what non-forgivers leave in their wake:

»   *Changed relationships.* They are never quite the same again, if left unreconciled. Proverbs is clear: "A brother offended is harder to be won than a strong city, and contentions are like the bars of a citadel" (18:19).

»   *Destroyed friendships.* This goes one step further. Instead of merely changing the *feel* of a relationship, non-forgivers will often *cease to maintain* the relationship at all. It totally disappears from the map! There is no effort at contact, no concern for well-being, and no regret from the absence. You can count on it: "He who conceals a transgression seeks love, but he who repeats a matter separates intimate friends" (Proverbs 17:9).

»   *Ministry casualties.* Sometimes the carnage of bitterness results in the break of a ministry partnership. How ironic: ministries *united* around the gospel *divide*! Paul and Barnabas were not immune to this (Acts 15:36–41). The two ministry-minded women Euodia and Syntyche were not immune to this (Philippians 4:2–3). Neither are we.

» *Personal isolation.* Getting burned one too many times can find us running to a quiet room and a dark corner. You don't want to be around people anymore because they may hurt you again. Your *trust* in others is gone. You look with suspicion at people in your past, mistrust people in your present, and are cynical about people in the future. Just remember, though, that being alone is never safe (Proverbs 18:1).

» *Withered fruit.* If you choose to be a non-forgiver, you will also pay the high price of stalling your growth into Christlikeness. Every believer enjoys the indwelling presence and ministry of the Holy Spirit (Romans 8:9–11; 2 Corinthians 3:18). The Spirit leaves an incredible footprint in each believer's life—"love, joy, peace, patience, kindness, goodness, faithfulness, gentleness, self-control" (Galatians 5:22–23). However, a non-forgiver stands *against* what the Spirit is working toward in his or her life.

» *Untamed tongues.* You might be the *nicest*

person in the church lobby on Sunday, but if you refuse to forgive someone, you are the *most violent* person in the church lobby. Jesus said that violence starts in the heart with hatred (Matthew 5:21–22). Gossip and slander are birthed in bitterness.

» *Unattractive witness.* All of the above yield in non-forgivers fruit that is inconsistent with the gospel's work in their lives as believers. This was Paul's concern as he deployed a church member to reconcile the two ladies in the Philippian church. He wrote, "I ask you also to help these women who have shared my struggle in the cause of the gospel, together with Clement also and the rest of my fellow workers, whose names are in the book of life" (Philippians 4:3).

Read through the list again: changed relationships, destroyed friendships, ministry casualties, personal isolation, withered fruit, untamed tongues, and unattractive witness. This is serious stuff! It's serious enough to do something about it. Life is too short. The gospel is too powerful. God's glory is too important to be content with anything less than forgiveness.

Get Packed

This is why I want to invite you to take a trip with me. With our traction strong in the text of Matthew 18, I want us to walk the "Pathway to Forgiveness" with Jesus. There are five stops on our journey:

» Stop 1: Admit your hesitancy

» Stop 2: Remember your story

» Stop 3: Guard your heart

» Stop 4: Fear your Lord

» Stop 5: Enact your forgiveness

I don't know who has wronged you. I don't know how far you must go to forgive someone. But I do know the *way* you will travel to get there. It's the same pathway our Lord outlined for his disciple Peter. It is timeless. It is sufficient. It is freeing. Here's my promise to you: if you complete this journey, you will find fresh resolve and abundant grace to be the forgiving disciple that Jesus Christ desires.

So let's begin our trip. Forgiving an offender in your life will be our final destination. Matthew 18 will serve as our GPS. Bring coffee.

1

Admit Your Hesitancy

It was another busy day of ministry. His reputation was spreading. Yet Christ's disciples were taking advantage of his growing popularity not for the sake of his kingdom but rather for their own little kingdoms. By the time we catch up with them in Matthew 18, they are crunched into a small home in Capernaum, probably Peter's home again (see Mark 1:29; 9:33). Their topic of discussion is not the grandeur of Jesus, the needs of the multitudes, the lessons they have been learning as disciples, or the plan to reach the world with the news of the King. Instead, it is summarized in a question they put to Jesus:

> Who then is greatest in the kingdom
> of heaven?
>
> (18:1)

They are riding his coattails to greatness and power.

Jesus Kids His Disciples

Christ loved them and loves us enough to save us from our own lust for winning and supremacy. He alone wins, and he alone is supreme (Colossians 1:15–18). Whenever we find ourselves wanting to grab what Christ alone enjoys, we are in danger. On this particular day in Capernaum, Jesus sets out to save his disciples from their own agendas of greatness. To do so, he reaches for the last person in the room that these guys would consider to be great:

> And He called a child to Himself and set him before them, and said, "Truly I say to you, unless you are converted and become like children, you will not enter the kingdom of heaven. Whoever then humbles himself as this child, he is the greatest in the kingdom of heaven. And whoever receives one such child in My name receives Me."
>
> (18:2–5)

Mark adds a detail in his account (Mark 9:36):

> Taking a child, He set him before

them, *and taking him in His arms...*
[emphasis added].

Jammed into a room full of ambitious, glory-
seeking disciples, Jesus looks past them all to a
young child, calls him to himself, takes him into
his arms, points to him and says, in essence, "If
you want to be *great*, be a childlike disciple like
this one I'm holding." He then goes on to explain
how precious all childlike disciples (of all ages)
are in his sight. Specifically, he is very protective
of them, and warns the disciples against leading
them into sin (vv. 6–11). Whenever any of his
childlike disciples do stray into sin, he personally
pursues them to restore them (vv. 12–14). Most
often he reaches for them through the loving
means of his church (vv. 15–20). The disciples want
greatness? What could be greater than content-
edly living under the care of the Great Shepherd ...
like a child?

Of course, it is Peter who speaks up first in
the living room that day. His mouth is always in
motion just a few moments before his thinking! He
has been tracking closely with the Lord's words,
especially the teaching about Christ's concern over
believers who sin against one another (v. 15). He
asks Jesus,

Lord, how often shall my brother sin
against me and I forgive him? Up to
seven times?

(v. 21)

Peter's question is incredible and very revealing.
In this one question, Peter gives expression to
every believer's major obstacle to granting forgiveness to those who have sinned against them to
any degree. We can make two observations about
Peter's words. Track carefully with me: Do you see
yourself here?

First, Peter was being *generous* with his question. "Why seven times?" you may wonder. We
need to give Peter a little credit here. He had
already been taught by Jesus to be forgiving.

For if you forgive others for their transgressions, your heavenly Father will also
forgive you. But if you do not forgive
others, then your Father will not forgive
your transgressions.

(6:14–15)

In reaching for the number seven, Peter was
actually more than doubling the "going rate" of
his day. The Jewish rabbis at that time believed

that God required someone to forgive an offender only three times (based on Amos 1–2). Peter was being quite generous, sincerely thinking that he was obeying Jesus' teaching. But before you take Peter's measurement for a new halo, let me point out one more detail.

Second, Peter was being *hesitant* with his question. Even though he used a larger number than those around him, don't miss the fact that he *was still keeping count*. Today, we would say that he played the game while watching the scoreboard. He still wanted limits in place as to how many times a person could sin against him. He knew nothing about what Paul would one day write:

> Love ... does not take into account a
> wrong suffered.
>
> (1 Corinthians 13:4–5)

Christlike love doesn't fixate on the scoreboard in friendships, marriages, families, or ministries.

The Risks of Forgiveness

The first stop on your Pathway to Forgiveness is to admit that you too are hesitant to forgive.

We all are—it's our default setting. While as a Christian you are saved from the penalty of being "unmerciful" (Romans 1:31), you still feel its gravity in your heart. Why? Honesty here will determine the success of the rest of your journey. There are basically four common fears that lobby against your forgiving someone when he or she asks you to do so.

The Fear of Insincerity

This fear cries out, "How can I know this person is sincere?" Perhaps the offender in your life has a long pattern of wronging you in a particular manner. Perhaps you have been hurt by others too deeply too often, even after they had asked your forgiveness multiple times. Perhaps the offender is faking a remorseful spirit. How *do* you know that the offender is sincere? The fact is, you *don't* know. Proverbs is painfully honest:

> A plan in the heart of a man is like
> deep water.
>
> (20:5; see also Psalm 64:6)

The good news, though, is that you don't have to answer for *the offender's sincerity*; you only have to answer for *your obedience.*[2]

THE FEAR OF VULNERABILITY

This fear reasons, "If I get soft, I'll get hurt." Is this a possibility? Yes. Is this a *bad* thing? No, because it will place you in good company with others whose obedience left them vulnerable to further hurts. Jesus had already taught this to Peter earlier:

> Blessed are the merciful, for they shall
> receive mercy ... Blessed are you when
> people insult you and persecute you, and
> falsely say all kinds of evil against you
> because of Me. Rejoice and be glad, for
> your reward in heaven is great; for in the
> same way they persecuted the prophets
> who were before you.
>
> (Matthew 5:7, 11–12)

Being a merciful person does make you an easy target who stands out from the rest, but you will stand shoulder-to-shoulder with the likes of Jeremiah, David, Jesus, and Paul!

---

2   True repentance will bring forth fruit in time
    (2 Corinthians 7:10–11). If the offender is a believer, the
    church may be needed to prod him or her toward fruit
    (Matthew 18:15-20).

THE FEAR OF CHANGE

The fact is, you may have gotten comfortable *not liking* the offender. You have figured out a way to "do life" without intersecting with this person, looking him or her in the eye, or being concerned for his or her well-being. In your comfort, you have resisted the idea of forgiveness because it will require that something comfortable become uncomfortable. But you must remember that Christ has Christlikeness as his agenda for your life (Romans 12:2; 2 Corinthians 3:18). The change he requires of you is *freeing* you to live out love, joy, peace, patience, kindness, goodness, faithfulness, gentleness, and self-control toward the very person who has wounded you (Galatians 5:22–23). Wow! That's *grace*.

THE FEAR OF EXPOSURE

It is possible that you either participated in the sin with the offender or reacted in sin to the offender. Beginning the transaction of forgiveness would bring to light the repentance that is required on your part for your words, actions, and attitudes. Up to this point, most people in your life who know of the wrong deed believe it was totally the offender's fault. Proverbs 18:17 is brutally honest:

> *The first to plead his case seems right,*
> *until another comes and examines him.*

The fact also remains that you could be wrong in your understanding of the offense as well.

> *Do not go out hastily to argue your case;*
> *otherwise, what will you do in the end,*
> *when your neighbor humiliates you?*
> (Proverbs 25:8)

Matthew Henry wrote long ago, "There is a proneness in our corrupt nature to stint ourselves in that which is good, and to be afraid of doing too much in religion, particularly of forgiving too much, though we have so much forgiven us."[3]

These four fears paralyze countless believers to hold back in forgiving. Yet I suggest that all these fears have one common denominator: *pride.* Somehow, somewhere, we find a way to make an offense all about *us.* So we keep count. When we move from Peter's question in Matthew 18:21 to Jesus' reply in verse 22, we not only change *speakers*; we also change *worldviews.*

---

3 Matthew Henry, *A Commentary on the Whole Bible*, vol. 5 (Old Tappan, NJ: Revell, [n.d.]), 263.

The Requirement of Christ

> Jesus said to him, "I do not say to you,
> up to seven times, but up to seventy
> times seven."
>
> (Matthew 18:22)

With these words and numbers Jesus is emphatically stating that his childlike disciples are not to keep count at all! His point is not that we should count up to 490 individual offenses by every possible offender. That would be impossible and ridiculous! Rather, it is that we put the calculator away and stop staring at the scoreboard. *He is indicating that it is possible to live on a higher plane than bitterness.*

At this point it is helpful to look at a very important parallel passage found in Luke 17:3-4, where Jesus teaches his disciples,

> Be on your guard! If your brother sins,
> rebuke him; and if he repents, forgive
> him. And if he sins against you seven
> times a day, and returns to you seven
> times, saying, "I repent," forgive him.

See his point? Jesus is teaching us that when it comes to others sinning against us, it is not to be a matter of *points* (i.e., keeping score). Rather, it is to be a matter of *posture*—being ready to forgive whenever the transaction of forgiveness presents itself to us, even if it is the same sin seven times in one day. The disciples clearly got the point, as evidenced by their response in the very next verse:

> *Increase our faith!*
>
> (v. 5)

It takes faith to be vulnerable, but the place of vulnerability is the safest place to be.

The Importance of Good Posture

What can we know about this posture of standing ready to forgive that Jesus prescribes for his disciples? A fourfold description will help you understand what he means.

1. IT IS COMMANDED

Jesus' words are not a suggestion.

> Whenever you stand praying, forgive, if
> you have anything against anyone, so that

your Father who is in heaven will also
forgive you your transgressions.

(Mark 11:25)

Our stance is to be ready to forgive instead of
ready to take revenge.

Do not say, "Thus I shall do to him as he
has done to me; I will render to the man
according to his work."

(Proverbs 24:29)

And this command to forgive is given by a forgiving
God, a fact that Jesus highlights when he says,

Be merciful, just as your Father is merciful.

(Luke 6:36)

2. IT MUST BE CONSTANT

Specifically, being ready to forgive is what you
carry into offenses, not what you *work up* after an
offense. It is the posture of your heart before the
offense even happens. Proverbs 19:11 states,

A man's discretion makes him slow to
anger, and it is his glory to overlook

a transgression.

(See also 16:32)

In the event that someone sins against you, you are armed and ready to retaliate with *good* (Romans 12:21).

3. *It Must be Cultivated*

The reality is that this stance *must* be developed in the life of every believer, and it can *only* be grown in the soil of trials and offenses. James writes,

> Consider it all joy, my brethren, when you
> encounter various trials, knowing that the
> testing of your faith produces endurance.
> And let endurance have its perfect result,
> so that you may be perfect and complete,
> lacking in nothing.
> (James 1:2–4; see also Romans 5:3–4)

It's worth the pain and vulnerability because the mature fruit will be amazing (Galatians 5:22–23).

4. *It Is Christlike*

The One who was more wronged than anyone else said these words from his cross:

Father, forgive them; for they do not
know what they are doing.

(Luke 23:34)

Though the crowd he was looking at were not regenerated in that moment at the cross but only later at Pentecost, Christ's heart posture was clear. Stephen (Acts 7:60) and Paul (2 Timothy 4:16) also sounded like their Lord during their ultimate trials. We have to ask a very serious question: Is it possible to grow in Christlikeness *at all* if we do not have a posture that is ready to forgive?

This first stop on our journey is a difficult one. Yet it is a necessary one. It explains to us why we have never gotten past this point before in forgiving others. It becomes our opportunity to deal with our own hearts and repent. And then the journey continues.

2

Remember Your Story

Perhaps it is Peter's perplexed look as he is calc-ulating seventy times seven. Jesus sees the need to illustrate just what a posture of forgiveness looks like. So he tells a story that will become the greatest, most timeless lesson on believers forgiving others.

> For this reason the kingdom of heaven
> may be compared to a king who wished to
> settle accounts with his slaves. When he
> had begun to settle them, one who owed
> him ten thousand talents was brought to
> him. But since he did not have the means
> to repay, his lord commanded him to be
> sold, along with his wife and children
> and all that he had, and repayment to be
> made. So the slave fell to the ground and
> prostrated himself before him, saying,
> "Have patience with me and I will repay
> you everything."
>
> (Matthew 18:23–26)

The setting which Jesus describes is most likely that of ancient regional governors giving an account of their financial activity to their Gentile king (v. 23). The scene takes only one verse to build to a tense one-on-one scene between the king and a certain governor-servant. The air is thick.

Hopeless Accountability

This was a *personal* debt. For some reason, this governor-servant's region had accumulated immense debt on his watch, and he was responsible for it. No other servant of the king would share in the blame—only he deserved it. It was only right for the king to look directly at his servant, who owed him so much.

This was an *incalculable* debt. Jesus was probably referring to the Attic Talent, which was used to weigh precious metals. Interestingly, Jesus also reached for the highest number in the Greek language—"ten thousand" (v. 24). How much was a talent worth? Six thousand denarii. A denarius was one day's wage. This is amazing! It would take one person six thousand working days to earn *one* talent—that's sixteen to eighteen years of work! In a lifetime, an average worker could earn only three or four talents. Yet this servant personally owed his king ten thousand talents. The amount is astronomical, out of sight, beyond mammoth. As we try to imagine this we are overwhelmed—right where Jesus wants us to be as the story continues.

This was an *unpayable* debt. In the ancient Gentile world, it was common for families to be forcibly sold into slavery in order to pay a debt (v. 25). The problem in this particular story was that, according to the going rate, selling the man's wife and children would bring in only between five hundred and two thousand days' wages—not even half of one talent. This debt was out of reach for repayment even to begin.

Finally, this was a *growing* debt. As with financial debt in our day, the passing of time with no payment only yielded a larger debt. Each day, more was owed. If we are overwhelmed with the concept of a ten-thousand-talent debt, we are even more blown away that it would continue to grow if nothing were done.

Are you feeling the hopeless accountability in this story that Jesus is telling to Peter and to any disciple who wants to keep score instead of maintaining a posture that is ready to forgive?

Desperate Agreement

With this mammoth unpayable debt weighing down on the servant-governor's shoulders, he made a simple reply to the charges (v. 26). Notice that he made no excuses for his debt, blaming his past experiences, difficult region, or personality quirks. He didn't blame anyone else, not even the king for being unreasonable and heartless. He denied nothing and accepted ownership of the horrific debt. He expected justice. He fell on his face and pleaded for mercy. Let his exact wording sink deep into your heart: "Have patience with me and I will repay you everything" (v. 26). Yeah, right. How, exactly?

Complete Acquittal

What happens next in this story shocks us. We are not expecting it. Jesus' disciples in that Capernaum home must gasp as Jesus continues,

> And the lord of that slave felt compassion
> and released him and forgave him
> the debt.

> (v. 27)

What! A debt that is beyond our mind's grasp is there one moment and then gone the next. How can this be? There is only one answer—it's all because of the will of the king. He dismisses the debt, sending it away. Just a moment ago we couldn't *see around* the obstacle (debt); now we can't even *see* it! The king alone has the right to have compassion on the servant, order the servant's release, and announce the debt's forgiveness. William MacDonald says of this scene, "It was an epic display of grace, not justice."[4]

Whose Story Is This?

If the ten-thousand-talent debt was *astronomical*, this act of mercy by the king toward this servant was *astounding*. What is Christ's main point here? Simply put, this is the story of an *unworthy servant forgiven an unpayable debt*.

But why *this* story? Why now? Catch the words Jesus used to open this illustration in 18:23: "For this reason the kingdom of heaven may be compared to ..."

While the ultimate expression of the kingdom of heaven will be a literal kingdom on earth in the

---

4   William MacDonald, *Believer's Bible Commentary*
     (Nashville: Thomas Nelson, 1995), 1274.

future, that very kingdom is being built now by Jesus in the hearts of men and women (Luke 17:21; Romans 14:17; Colossians 1:13). What is unseen now will be fully manifested in the future, when Jesus returns to sit on David's throne on the earth (Matthew 25:31; Revelation 20:1–7). So when Jesus introduces this story with a comparison with life in the kingdom of heaven, he is referring to the time when his kingdom is being built by him, the King, in the hearts of his people now. He is saying that the scorekeeping is a common reality in the hearts of his people during the time between his two advents—the time in which Peter lived *and we live*! This story is given as a gift to anyone who struggles to forgive instead of maintaining a posture that is ready to forgive.

There is one more reality about this story that we must notice. So far, you have been in the audience in this king's palace. You have gasped with everyone else to hear the enormity of the ten-thousand-talent debt that this one servant-governor personally owed. Even more, you have marveled at the king's mercy—forgiving such an unworthy servant such an unpayable debt. Now you step out from the onlookers and approach this servant, who is still face down on the ground before the forgiving king. As the servant stands to his feet

upon hearing of the cancellation of his enormous
debt, he turns to look at you. And you are shocked!
As you look at his face, you immediately recognize
it. *It is you.* This is *your* story. It is the gospel's
collision with *your* life. The unpayable debt was
yours, and the unworthy servant is *you*. This is
the second stop on your Pathway to Forgiveness—
"Remember your story." As you go back over this
story in your mind, three specific questions will
effectively help you remember that you are reading
details about *yourself*.

1. Was *Your* Accountability Hopeless?

Your answer, without qualifier, is "Yes." Your debt
was a *personal* debt—a debt you had to answer for
one-on-one with the King. There was no avoiding
it, denying it, or escaping it.

> *God will bring every act to judgment,*
> *everything which is hidden, whether it is*
> *good or evil.*
> (Ecclesiastes 12:14; see also Hebrews 9:27)

Your debt was an *incalculable* debt. Left to
yourself, your appointment in the King's hall
would have been devastating—ten thousand tal-

ents devastating. Even worse, your debt to the King was not one of *currency*; it was one of *piracy*:

> For all have sinned and fall short of the
> glory of God.
>
> (Romans 3:23)

Not only did your King announce your debt to you; he could not even look at it. His gaze burned right through you.

> For You are not a God who takes pleasure
> in wickedness; no evil dwells with You.
> The boastful shall not stand before Your
> eyes; You hate all who do iniquity.
>
> (Psalm 5:4–5)

Your debt was an *unpayable* debt. Since you could not even begin to pay back your debt, you were doomed.

> The LORD will by no means leave the
> guilty unpunished.
>
> (Nahum 1:3; see also Exodus 34:7)

A ten-thousand-talent debt would have been far easier to handle than your sin-debt. Much easier.

Finally, your debt was a *growing* debt. If nothing changed, it would only grow greater and greater with the passing of time. The Bible is clear that Jesus is building three realities during this age: his church (Matthew 16:18), his heaven (John 14:2–3), and his *wrath* (2 Thessalonians 1:7–9; Acts 17:30–31). A lack of awareness of this is a dangerous oversight. Eternally.

2. Was *Your* Agreement Desperate?

Your answer, without a qualifier, is "Yes" again. When the King opened your eyes to the enormity of your sin-debt, you realized that you were indeed poor in spirit, and you mourned your condition (Matthew 5:3–4). To borrow King David's words, you cried out,

> I know my transgressions, and my sin is ever before me. Against You, You only, I have sinned and done what is evil in Your sight, so that You are justified when You speak and blameless when You judge.
> (Psalm 51:3–4)

There are no excuses, no blaming others, no denial. There is only an admission of debt, an expectation of justice, and pleading for mercy. Desperation always cries out for mercy.

3. Was *Your* Acquittal Complete?

Your answer, without qualifier, is a glorious "Yes!" Your ten-thousand-talent debt that was there one moment was eternally gone the next, all because of the will and mercy of the King! And when the Bible states that it is *gone*, it means:

» *Your sin is never to be met again.* "As far as the east is from the west, so far has He removed our transgressions from us" (Psalm 103:12).

» *Your sin is never to be seen again.* "It is You who has kept my soul from the pit of nothingness, for You have cast all my sins behind Your back" (Isaiah 38:17).

» *Your sin is never to be found again.* "He will again have compassion on us; He will tread our iniquities under foot. Yes, You will cast all their sins into the depths of the sea" (Micah 7:19).

» *Your sin is never to be read again.* "I, even I, am the one who wipes out your transgressions for My own sake, and I will not

remember your sins" (Isaiah 43:25; see also
Colossians 2:13–15).

But here is where your story differs from that of
the governor-servant in Jesus' story. *Your debt was
fully paid.*

> He made Him who knew no sin to be sin
> on our behalf, so that we might become
> the righteousness of God in Him.
>   (2 Corinthians 5:21)

Never miss this stop on your Pathway to Forgiveness. If you do not remember your story constantly,
you will never be able to forgive anyone anything.
Period. Gospel-amnesia yields a life of bitterness;
gospel-treasuring yields a posture of forgiveness.

One more question: *Is* this your story? If you
have never repented of your sin and cried out to
Jesus to be your Lord and Savior, you can do that
right now! Place your faith in Him *alone*. John 1:12
cannot be any clearer:

> But as many as received Him, to them He
> gave the right to become children of God,
> even to those who believe in His name.[5]

---

5 Take time to visit The Story, at http://viewthestory.com.

3

Guard Your Heart

This story from Jesus would be a great story if it ended right here—an unworthy servant forgiven an unpayable debt. Sadly, this story is only getting started. Remember that Jesus' purpose in telling this story to Peter is to correct his unwillingness to forgive in a way that is consistent with the gospel. As Jesus continues the story, things get ugly fast. We now find out that this servant has debt-amnesia almost immediately. What comes out of his heart now is horrific. A sobering question you need to ask yourself is, "Do I recognize this?" When you are wronged, does what comes out of your heart look anything like what comes out of this servant? It's a hard question, but it is the third necessary stop on your Pathway to Forgiveness. Note the four timeless characteristics of the non-forgiver.

1. Mirrored Reaction of the World

> But that slave went out and found one of
> his fellow slaves who owed him a hundred

> denarii; and he seized him and began
> to choke him, saying, "Pay back what
> you owe."
>
> (Matthew 18:28)

I am floored when I read this. Such anger from out of nowhere! Actually, his anger and bitterness were there all the time. What we should be more surprised at is the tenderness he had just demonstrated in the king's throne room moments before this. The rage he now demonstrated was always in his heart.

> Watch over your heart with all diligence,
> for from it flow the springs of life.
>
> (Proverbs 4:23;
> see also 23:7; Ecclesiastes 7:9)

Mark it down: bitterness and anger in our hearts will *always* eventually surface, and this will most often happen when we are sinned against. The book of Proverbs guarantees this:

» Proverbs 29:22: "An angry man stirs up strife, and a hot-tempered man abounds in transgression."

» Proverbs 12:16: "A fool's anger is known at once."

» Proverbs 27:4: "Wrath is fierce and anger is a flood."

This governor-servant's anger against his fellow servant immediately escalated into a physical attack. His fingers were on the guy's throat! This is known as "debt-violence" and it was very common in that day. According to one biblical scholar, "Creditors often dragged their debtors before the judge, as the Roman law allowed them to, holding them by the throat."[6] Bitterness always reveals mercy-amnesia.

This is how the world responds to both *actual* and *perceived* offenses—through *reaction*. Sadly, we don't have to be taught to react this way when others sin against us; it is part of our natural wiring (Romans 1:19–31). We may not go for their throats (physical assault), but we often respond with:

» *Verbal assault:* This shows up in how we talk *to* them and *about* them. Our words become like weapons we use to pulverize them (Proverbs 12:18; Psalm 57:4).

» *Social assault:* This shows up as we seek to isolate them from others, or we start to divide

6 Marvin Vincent, *Word Studies*, vol. 1 (Peabody, MA: Hendrickson, [n.d.]), 106.

our mutual acquaintances into "teams"—
those who are "with us" and those who are
"with them." We actually become social
terrorists in their lives (Proverbs 16:28).

» *Motive assault:* This shows up when we really
believe we can read their heart motivations.
We begin to question everything they ever do
(past, present, future). This is the death of
trust in the relationship (1 Corinthians 4:3–5).

2. Skewed Perspective of Offenses

The second characteristic of a non-forgiver is that
he or she really believes that *to wrong* is human,
but *to be wronged* is catastrophic! Recall from
Jesus' story that this governor-servant's debt to
the king was ten thousand talents, with one talent
equaling six thousand denarii (sixteen to eighteen
years' wages). Yet the debt that was owed him from
a fellow servant was only a hundred denarii—a
mere grain of sand in a dump truck compared
with the debt he himself owed at one time! This
comparison is staggering, and it reveals that,
like the first servant, Peter and all scorekeepers
who refuse to maintain a posture ready to forgive
believe two simple lies every day.

Lie 1: Big Is Little

In short, non-forgivers have lost sight of the enormity of their ten-thousand-talent sin-debt that was forgiven them by God through Christ. If you believe that you *can't* or *don't have to* forgive someone who asks for your forgiveness, you are no longer looking at life through the lens of the gospel. John 3:16 no longer sings to you. You effectively live life as if your big sin-debt was little.

Lie 2: Little Is Big

Non-forgivers insist that the offenses on the horizontal human level are of greater importance than the vertical forgiveness they have received in Christ. A hundred denarii was basically worth a mere three months' wages—pennies compared with the first debt. I want to be lovingly bold when I say that the *worst* sin that could be committed against you in this life (whether in marriage, ministry, families, etc.), though extreme, is only a hundred denarii in comparison with your sin which Christ forgave you at salvation. Commentator Lenski notes that both debts are real; one is *payable*, while the other is *unpayable*.[7]

---

7   R. C. H. Lenski, *Matthew: Commentary on the New Testament* (Peabody, MA: Hendrickson, 1998), 718.

3. Short Memory of Mercy

Just when we think the story cannot get any more traumatic, we hear a haunting conversation between the two servants:

> So his fellow slave fell to the ground and began to plead with him, saying, "Have patience with me and I will repay you." But he was unwilling ...
>
> (18:29–30a)

Did you catch that? This desperate plea is word-for-word the same plea that the first servant cried out to the king at 18:26! Furthermore, the Greek indicates that it was a persistent pleading met with a relentless refusal. The pace of this story seems to also communicate that only a very short time had passed since 18:26, possibly only minutes! The same words met with two different responses. Charles Spurgeon marvels, "Just now he was a *lowly suppliant*, but now he is a *hectoring tyrant*!"[8] The problem with this first servant, and with Peter—and with us, when we struggle to maintain a posture that is ready to forgive—is twofold.

---

8   Charles Spurgeon, *Matthew: The King Has Come*, ed. Larry Richards (Old Tappan, NJ: Revell, 1987), 256.

First, there is a *failure to understand the doctrine*. When we don't stand ready to forgive, we have yet to grasp the guilt that was removed from us (i.e., forgiveness). We have yet to grasp the debt that was absorbed by Christ (atonement). We have yet to grasp the relationship that was restored with God (reconciliation). We have yet to grasp the declaration that was issued by God (justification). We have yet to grasp the motivation that was revealed (grace).

Second, there is a *failure to revisit the scene.* Whenever the ten-thousand-talent servant sat daydreaming, his thoughts should have taken him back to the king's hall, where he only a short time before had heard, "Release him, and forgive his debt." Likewise, we are never to forget the unpayable debt that was forgiven us, unworthy servants. The apostle Paul never got over it:

> I was formerly a blasphemer and a
> persecutor and a violent aggressor. Yet
> I was shown mercy because I acted
> ignorantly in unbelief; and the grace of
> our Lord was more than abundant, with
> the faith and love which are found in
> Christ Jesus.
>
> (1 Timothy 1:13–14)

4. Quiet Desire for the Offender's Suffering

Verse 30 takes us to a new depth in this sad story:

> *But he was unwilling and went and threw him in prison until he should pay back what was owed.*[9]

What an unreasonable expectation! How was this servant supposed to work and pay off his three-month debt while he was locked up in prison? What an undeniable agenda: like all non-forgivers, *he had no plans to forgive at all!* There's a certain gospel-inconsistent joy in placing yourself *over* an offender in greatness rather than *beside* him or her as an equal (i.e., fellow servant). There is even an unspoken joy in having people *owe* you; making them suffer (remain in debt) puts you on top. The sad reality is that the offender's debt to you is ultimately a debt to *God*, since he is over both of you.

Does what comes out of this servant's heart look anything like what comes out of your heart when

---

9 Prison was the only option, since selling him into slavery would have brought in 500 denarii, while the debt was only 100 denarii.

you are sinned against? If so, this is where your repentance must begin.

> *He who conceals his transgressions will*
> *not prosper, but he who confesses and*
> *forsakes them will find compassion.*
>   (Proverbs 28:13)

It could be that this very stop on your Pathway to Forgiveness may finally open your eyes to what is holding you back from being always ready to forgive as Christ prescribes and as God has forgiven you.

4

Fear Your Lord

It is very possible that a believer can come this far on the journey and still lean toward being a non-forgiver. The servant in our story was forgiven so much only moments before, yet he still immediately chose to show no mercy to his fellow servant. When mercy is spurned and eclipsed like this in the stance of believers toward those who have wronged them, they stand in a very vulnerable, dangerous place. You must make a fourth stop on your journey if you are tempted to do the same—"Fear your Lord." Perhaps the three realities you see here will move you toward a forgiving posture.

You Will Face God's People

Jesus continues,

> So when his fellow slaves saw what had
> happened, they were deeply grieved and
> came and reported to their lord all that

had happened.

(Matthew 18:31)

No longer was the debt between these two servants a private matter. This display of non-mercy would spill over to other people. It always does.

The fact is that *you will stand out as an unforgiving person in a forgiving community.* It's interesting to see the response of the other fellow servants: "They were deeply grieved" (v. 31). Other believers *will* notice the bitterness and the breakdown in the application of the gospel's commands in your life if you are irreconcilable. They have known forgiveness in their own lives, and they treasure it in "the family." Even more, they know that *you* have been forgiven a ten-thousand-talent sin-debt by your King, yet you refuse to forgive a "lesser" sin-debt. It crushes other believers to see bitterness. Anyone who knows Ephesians 4:32—"Be kind to one another, tender-hearted, forgiving each other, just as God in Christ also has forgiven you"—will notice the profound breakdown between *your story* and *your bitterness.*

The fact is, *you will show up in believers' prayers.* The fellow servants "came and reported to their lord all that had happened" (v. 31). The onlookers didn't know what else to do but to approach their king on behalf of their fellow servant. They cried out to him in clarity and detail about the tragedy of a lack of mercy on the part of the ten-thousand-talent servant. They were greatly burdened about the inconsistency of this servant, the suffering of his fellow servant, and the testimony of the merciful king. So it is today: believers speak to the King with great urgency whenever forgiven people don't forgive. It's a pretty sobering reality, isn't it? If you are bitter, God's people somewhere are pouring out their hearts in prayer to God over your situation. And the King always listens.

You Will Face God's Rebuke

You can't miss the *accountability*. We are back in the king's hall. It should look familiar: we were here just a few moments ago with this same servant at 18:23–27. It's one-on-one again. The scene is kind of tense again. The air is thick. You could hear a needle drop and bounce off the marble floor—crystal clear.

> Then summoning him, his lord said to him, "You wicked slave, I forgave you all that debt because you pleaded with me.

*Should you not also have had mercy on
your fellow slave, in the same way that I
had mercy on you?"*

(v. 32-33)

Here's the truth for Peter and for us: if we
maintain a stance of non-forgiveness, we are now
an offense to our forgiving King! We answer to
him for how we respond to the offenses of others
against us. Paul reminds every believer,

*For we must all appear before the
judgment seat of Christ, so that each one
may be recompensed for his deeds in the
body, according to what he has done,
whether good or bad.*

(2 Corinthians 5:10)

You can't miss the *accusation*. Did you catch
the word that describes someone who isn't willing
to forgive? "Wicked" (v. 32). Literally, it means
hurtful and vicious! In the original Greek, the
same word is even used to describe the devil
himself (John 17:15; Ephesians 6:16; 1 John 2:13). It's
not a team uniform that any child of God should
desire to wear.

You can't miss the *expectation*. When you and I

won't forgive, our King shakes his head and says, "Your story paves the way for you to be a forgiver." In verse 32 the phrase "all that debt" is in an emphatic position in the Greek. The King also says to us, "Your brother belongs to *me*, not to you." Here in verse 33 we see the term "fellow slave" for the fourth time in this story (vv. 28–29, 31) to make this very point. Whoever has sinned against you has ultimately sinned against God, not just against you. Fellow servants answer ultimately to the same King. Finally, the King also says to you, "Your mercy reflects my mercy": "Should you not also have had mercy on your fellow slave, in the same way that I had mercy on you?" (18:33). The question itself penetrates with the gospel right to the heart of the non-forgiver. What Jesus is teaching Peter and us is that if we *ever* forget these truths, we cannot demonstrate true forgiveness toward others. Paul agrees, telling the Colossians that they should be

> ... bearing with one another, and forgiving each other, whoever has a complaint against anyone; just as the Lord forgave you, so also should you.
>
> (Colossians 3:13)

You Will Face God's Discipline

This sad story ends in the dungeon.

> And his lord, moved with anger, handed
> him over to the torturers until he should
> repay all that was owed him.
>
> (18:34)

We can conclude that this is *not* talking about losing one's salvation; the Bible is crystal clear that a truly saved person cannot become unsaved again (Romans 8:28–30; John 6:37; 10:27–30). It is interesting to note that the word used here is "torturer," not "executioner." The point Jesus is making is that the non-forgiver actually suffers more than the people whom he or she refuses to forgive. What irony! Jesus loves us so much that he mercifully steps in when we are bitter and goes to any length necessary to free us from its poison!

> God deals with you as with sons ... He
> disciplines us for our good, so that we
> may share His holiness.
>
> (Hebrews 12:7, 10;
> see also 1 Corinthians 11:32)

Some of the "torturers" for non-forgivers include:

» Gnawing guilt over your reaction and bitterness

» Physical illness possibly caused by your internalized stress and anger every day

» Unpleasant consequences as a result of your bitterness

» Loss of social freedom as you become a recluse who refuses to get hurt again

» Church discipline in obedience to Matthew 18:15–18

Warren Wiersbe writes,

The world's worst prison is the prison of an unforgiving heart. If we refuse to forgive others, then we are imprisoning ourselves and causing our own torment. Some of the most miserable people I have met in my ministry have been people who would not forgive others. They lived only to imagine ways to punish these people who had wronged them. But they were really only punishing themselves.[10]

When you and I were forgiven by God for our ten-thousand-talent sin-debt, we incurred a *brand new debt*: to be willing to forgive others. The question you need to answer is this: Where will *your* story end? At verse 27 or verse 34? Christ's warning is clear:

> My heavenly Father will also do the same to you, if each of you does not forgive his brother from your heart.
>
> (Matthew 18:35)

Only after this stop on your journey are you ready for the final destination.

---

10 Warren Wiersbe, *Bible Exposition Commentary*, vol. 1 (Wheaton, IL: Victor, 1989), 67.

Conclusion:
Enact Your Forgiveness

Biblical forgiveness is a *transaction*. You are ready to enter the transaction once you have walked with Jesus and Peter through this story and established a sincere posture that is ready to forgive. Once you have prayerfully and sincerely made the four previous stops on this Pathway to Forgiveness, you are ready to arrive at your fifth and final stop (the destination)—granting forgiveness to those who seek it from you (18:21–22; Luke 17:3–4).

Wisdom Needed for Forgiveness

When you have been sinned against you have two options: to either *lovingly cover* or *lovingly confront*. Are you to push for repentance and forgiveness for every possible offense, suspicion, slight, look, word, or silence? No. I believe that

there is such a thing as *unilateral covering*—
choosing not to consider an offense "holdable." Jay
Adams agrees:

> *"But," you ask, "must one go to another
> about every offense? Must there be
> rebuking, repenting, and forgiving over
> everything that happens?" ... A good
> question. No. God has provided a means
> for handling the multitude of offenses that
> we commit against one another. But it is
> not forgiveness ... It is only those sins that
> throw the covers off that must be dealt
> with by the Luke 17/Matthew 18 processes:
> those offenses that break fellowship and
> lead to an unreconciled condition require
> forgiveness. Otherwise, we simply learn to
> overlook a multitude of offenses against
> ourselves, recognizing that we are all
> sinners and that we must gratefully thank
> others for covering our sins as well.*[11]

The three main verses that explain what it
means to *lovingly cover* are:

» "Above all, keep fervent in your love for one

11 Adams, *From Forgiven to Forgiving*, 34.

another, because love covers a multitude of
sins" (1 Peter 4:8).

» "Hatred stirs up strife, but love covers all
   transgressions" (Proverbs 10:12).

» "He who conceals a transgression seeks love"
   (Proverbs 17:9).

In short, if you choose to lovingly cover an offense,
you will later say, "What offense?"

It's a serious thing to not hold an offense
against someone; it takes prayerful consideration
for wisdom as to whether your option in a particular case is to lovingly cover or to lovingly
confront. Specifically:

» *Confrontation is needed if the relationship
   is broken.* If there is a noticeable change in
   time spent together, speech used toward
   each other, or concern over each other's
   spiritual growth, you must go to the offender
   (Matthew 18:15).

» *Confrontation is needed if it is a serious
   offense against someone else.* "Love covering"
   is applicable only to offenses committed
   against yourself. If the offender is causing
   other believers to sin either directly, by

example, or through divisive behavior, you
must go to him or her (Matthew 18:6–7;
1 Corinthians 5:6).

» *Confrontation is needed if the offender is in
danger.* If the offender's path is destructive,
physically or spiritually, in his or her
fellowship with God, you must go to him or
her. James commissions believers to pursue
other believers who are acting in an unsaved
manner: "My brethren, if any among you
strays from the truth and one turns him back,
let him know that he who turns a sinner from
the error of his way will save his soul from
death and will cover a multitude of sins"
(James 5:19–20; see also Galatians 6:1).[12]

Promises Made During Forgiveness

If you prayerfully and biblically reach the con-
clusion that you must *lovingly confront*, you are
now entering the transaction of forgiveness. If
the offending brother or sister hears your loving
confrontation and responds with "Will you forgive
me?" you will be in the place to complete the

---

12 For these points I am indebted to John MacArthur,
The Freedom and Power of Forgiveness (Wheaton, IL:
Crossway, 1998), 128–134.

transaction by, in essence, making three promises when you say "I forgive you." The promises are clear:[13]

"I PROMISE I WILL NOT HOLD THIS OFFENSE IN MY HEART"
This is a choice of meditation: you will not meditate upon and worry over this offense. It is precisely here that you get to be different from the servant in Jesus' story; you get to extend the same forgiveness that you have experienced from your King!

> Be kind to one another, tender-hearted,
> forgiving each other, just as God in Christ
> also has forgiven you.
>
> (Ephesians 4:32)

I love what Jay Adams notes: "*Forgetting* is passive; *Not remembering* is active."[14] Every time you are tempted to meditate on a forgiven wrong committed by someone else, overcome these thoughts by meditating on the forgiveness Christ secured for you. Do you remember how *your* sin

---

13 For these points I am indebted to Ken Sande, *The Peacemaker: A Biblical Guide to Resolving Personal Conflict* (Grand Rapids: Baker, 1997), 188–190.

14 Adams, *From Forgiven to Forgiving*, 12.

was forgiven (Ch. 2)? God has promised you that it will never be met, seen, found, or read again.

"I Promise I Will Not Spread This Around to Others"

You will not bring this offense before others through gossip or slander in any format such as prayer meetings, texting, social media, or personal conversations.

> The words of a whisperer are like dainty morsels, and they go down into the innermost parts of the body.
>
> (Proverbs 18:8)

"I Promise I Will Not Bring This Up Against You"

The offense never again needs to be a topic of discussion, unless only to thank Christ for his grace in the transaction.

> He who repeats a matter separates intimate friends.
>
> (Proverbs 17:9)

These are heavy promises! Biblical forgiveness is humbling for all involved—humbling in confronting, humbling in asking for forgiveness, and humbling in actually forgiving. But they are also heavy promises for the simple reason that if you break any of these three promises, *you are the new offender*. When you promise, deliver by God's grace.

> Let your statement be, "Yes, yes" or "No, no"; anything beyond these is of evil.
> (Matthew 5:37)

Goals Pursued in Forgiveness

By this point you are winded from the journey as well as sobered by the weight of forgiveness. It is gospel *work* requiring a spiritual *sweat*! But it is definitely worth it all.

When you forgive, *you put God's glory on display*. Specifically, you shine a bright spotlight on the grace of Christ in salvation, as we saw in Jesus' story (Matthew 18:32–33). It's one thing to *talk* about Christ's forgiveness, but it's quite another thing to *demonstrate* it. I once had a friend who was selling a particular brand of kitchen knives. He told me over and over how sharp his knives were, yet I remained unimpressed. But when he pulled out thick pieces of leather and one-inch-thick rope and proceeded to pull the knives effortlessly through them all, I was sold! So it is with forgiveness. The greater the offense forgiven, the greater the display of the gospel!

When you forgive, *you promote the other person's Christlikeness.* Have you ever stopped to consider that the whole transaction of forgiveness is actually a means by which Christ will mature you both in your growth into his likeness?

> And we know that God causes all things
> to work together for good to those
> who love God, to those who are called
> according to His purpose.
>
> (Romans 8:28)

When you initiate reconciliation, you are actually discipling another believer.

> Let us consider how to stimulate one
> another to love and good deeds.
>
> (Hebrews 10:24)

Finally, when you forgive, *you prove your love for God.* Jesus taught that the greatest commandment given to us is to

> Love the Lord your God with all your
> heart, and with all your soul, and with all

your mind.

(Matthew 22:37)

And he also taught us what the greatest expression of this love is:

If you love Me, you will keep
My commandments.

(John 14:15)

Forgiveness, then, is really worship!

Hold On to This Map

The first time I drove my Chevrolet Nova from Detroit to Buffalo, as a young sixteen-year-old, I needed a map with very clear directions. I had no idea how to get there without them! I needed a map for the first couple of times I took that trip until I became familiar with the scenery, roads, landmarks, and route. It's the same with Matthew 18:21–35. Forgiveness is most often a difficult journey, but the route is clear. It finds its traction in the gospel that you yourself have tasted. But it is worth the trip. And the more you see the grace of Christ at work in your heart as you forgive, the easier the trip will get each time.

Personal Application Projects

1. Admit Your Hesitancy

   a. Which of the fears listed in Chapter 1 can you personally relate to? Why? Contrast these with Romans 12:14–21.

   b. In your own words, describe the posture that Christ requires.

2. Remember Your Story

   a. Who is the servant in the story in Matthew 18? Why is this significant for Peter and you?

   b. Describe the forgiveness you have experienced in salvation. In your own words, describe Paul's astonishment over his own story in 1 Timothy 1:12–17.

3. Guard Your Heart

   a. Describe each of the four characteristics of non-forgivers listed in Chapter 3 in your own words. Search out at least two Bible verses that describe each one.

   b. Which characteristic(s) can you relate to? Why?

4. Fear Your Lord

   a. Why does an unforgiving believer not make sense? Write out Ephesians 4:32 and Colossians 3:13.

   b. How can non-forgivers suffer more than the people who have wronged them?

5. Enact Your Forgiveness

   a. In your own words, explain the difference between lovingly covering and lovingly confronting.

   b. Why is the journey of forgiveness so valuable to you as a believer? How does 1 Timothy 4:7–10 apply to this journey?

Where Can I Get More Help?

BOOKS

Adams, Jay, *From Forgiven to Forgiving: Learning to Forgive One Another God's Way* (Amityville, NY: Calvary Press, 1994)

Brauns, Chris, *Unpacking Forgiveness: Biblical Answers for Complex Questions and Deep Wounds* (Wheaton, IL: Crossway, 2008)

MacArthur, John, *The Freedom and Power of Forgiveness* (Wheaton, IL: Crossway, 2009)

Sande, Ken, *The Peacemaker: A Biblical Guide to Resolving Personal Conflict* (Grand Rapids: Baker, 2004)

ARTICLES

Crater, Tim, "Counsel on Being Reconciled to Our Brother," in *Journal of Pastoral Practice*, 5/3 (1982), 25–34

Lane, Tim, "Pursuing and Granting Forgiveness," in *Journal of Biblical Counseling*, 23/2 (2005), 52–59

WEB SITES

Peacemaker Ministries: www.hispeace.org

Christian Counseling Education Foundation: www.ccef.org

Books in the Help! series include...

Help! He's Struggling with Pornography

Help! Someone I Love Has Been Abused

Help! My Toddler Rules the House

Help! Someone I Love Has Cancer

Help! I Want to Change

Help! My Spouse Has Been Unfaithful

Help! Someone I Love Has Alzheimer's

Help! I Have Breast Cancer

Help! I'm a Slave to Food

Help! My Teen Struggles With Same-Sex Attractions

Help! She's Struggling With Pornography

Help! I Can't Get Motivated

Help! I'm a Single Mom

Help! I'm Confused About Dating

Help! I'm Drowning in Debt

Help! My Teen is Rebellious

Help! I'm Depressed

Help! I'm Living With Terminal Illness

Help! I Feel Ashamed

Help! I Want to Model Submission in Marriage

Help! I Can't Handle All These Trials

Help! I Can't Forgive

Help! My Anger is Out of Control

Help! My Friend is Suicidal

Help! I'm in a Conflict

Help! I'm Being Deployed

Help! I've Been Traumatized by Combat

Help! I'm So Lonely

Help! My Kids Are Viewing Porn

Help! I Need a Church

More titles in preparation

For current listing go to: www.shepherdpress.com/lifeline